Tiffany

The Charles Hosmer Morse Museum of American Art

A BOOK OF POSTCARDS

Pomegranate

SAN FRANCISCO

Pomegranate Communications, Inc.
Box 6099
Rohnert Park, CA 94927
www.pomegranate.com

Pomegranate Europe Ltd.
Fullbridge House, Fullbridge
Maldon, Essex CM9 4LE
England

ISBN 0-7649-0943-6
Pomegranate Catalog No. A944

Pomegranate publishes books of
postcards on a wide range of subjects.
Please write to the publisher for more information.

Designed by Shannon Lemme
Printed in Hong Kong
08 07 06 05 04 03 02 01 00   10 9 8 7 6 5 4 3

To facilitate detachment of the postcards from this book, fold each card along its perforation line before tearing.

The work of Louis Comfort Tiffany (1848–1933) enjoyed an international reputation at the turn of the twentieth century. At the turn of the twenty-first century, his innovation in the creation of leaded-glass windows, blown glass, mosaics, lamps, and jewelry has perhaps eclipsed the appeal of his work a century ago, capturing the interest of serious collectors and scholars as well, and assuring him a place in art history.

The son of Charles Lewis Tiffany, who founded the jewelry store Tiffany and Co., Louis Comfort Tiffany began his artistic career as a painter. When he was still a young man he headed an interior design firm that listed such influential clients as President Chester A. Arthur, Mark Twain, Cornelius Vanderbilt II, and Louisine and Henry O. Havemeyer. The firm was to launch his explorations in virtually all media, and later he founded Tiffany Studios, staffed by skilled artists and artisans who created works under his direction. There he developed his lustrous Favrile glass. Showing works at international expositions, he won medals from over the world.

This selection of thirty full-color images of Tiffany's work in various media is from the collection of The Charles Hosmer Morse Museum of American Art in Winter Park, Florida. The collection, built over fifty years by Hugh and Jeannette McKean, has been called the most comprehensive in the world. It includes the exquisite Byzantine-Romanesque-inspired chapel that Tiffany designed for the 1893 World's Columbian Exposition. For the first time in more than a century, the chapel was opened in early 1999 to be seen by the public as Tiffany had originally intended.

The Charles Hosmer Morse
Museum of American Art

Daffodils window, 1900
Louis Comfort Tiffany (1848–1933)
Leaded Favrile glass

Pomegranate

BOX 6099, ROHNERT PARK, CA 94927

Tiffany

The Charles Hosmer Morse Museum of American Art

Peony table lamp, c. 1902
Louis Comfort Tiffany (1848-1933)
Tiffany Studios, New York
Leaded Favrile glass

Pomegranate BOX 6099, ROHNERT PARK, CA 94927

Tiffany

The Charles Hosmer Morse
Museum of American Art

Landscape with Peacock and Peonies window, 1900–1910
Louis Comfort Tiffany (1848–1933)
Tiffany Studios, New York
Leaded Favrile glass

Pomegranate

BOX 6099, ROHNERT PARK, CA 94927

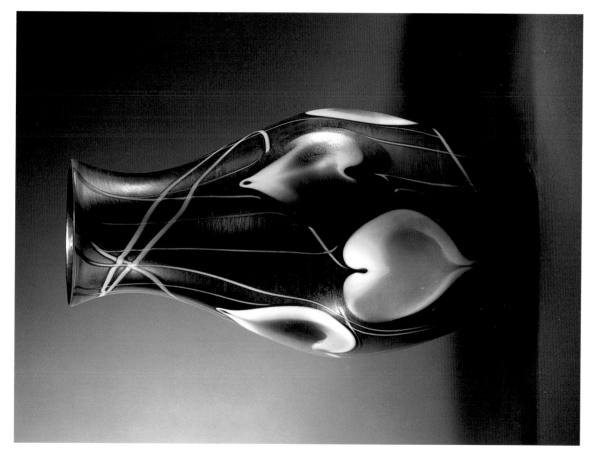

Tiffany

The Charles Hosmer Morse
Museum of American Art

Floriform vase, 1907
Louis Comfort Tiffany (1848–1933)
Blown Favrile glass

BOX 6099, ROHNERT PARK, CA 94927

Pomegranate

Tiffany — The Charles Hosmer Morse
Museum of American Art

Door Panels for the Heckscher House, c. 1904
Louis Comfort Tiffany (1848–1933)
Favrile glass, 122"x 135"

Pomegranate

BOX 6099, ROHNERT PARK, CA 94927

Tiffany

The Charles Hosmer Morse
Museum of American Art

Four Seasons gold box, c. 1914
After Louis Comfort Tiffany's *Four Seasons* windows
Tiffany & Company, New York

Pomegranate · BOX 6099, ROHNERT PARK, CA 94927

Tiffany The Charles Hosmer Morse
Museum of American Art

Feeding the Flamingos window, c. 1892
Designed by Louis Comfort Tiffany (1848–1933)
Tiffany Glass & Decorating Co., New York
Leaded Favrile glass

Pomegranate BOX 6099, ROHNERT PARK, CA 94927

Tiffany

The Charles Hosmer Morse
Museum of American Art

Magnolia window, c. 1885
Louis Comfort Tiffany (1848–1933)
Tiffany Glass Company, New York
Leaded Favrile glass

Pomegranate

BOX 6099, ROHNERT PARK, CA 94927

Tiffany

The Charles Hosmer Morse
Museum of American Art

Detail from *Grape Arbor* window, after 1908
Tiffany Studios, New York
Leaded Favrile glass

BOX 6099, ROHNERT PARK, CA 94927

Pomegranate

The Charles Hosmer Morse
Museum of American Art

Rose window, c. 1906
Tiffany Studios, New York
Leaded Favrile glass

Pomegranate   BOX 6099, ROHNERT PARK, CA 94927

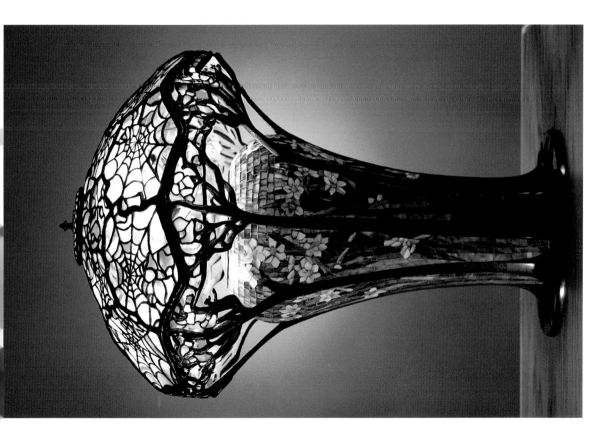

The Charles Hosmer Morse Museum of American Art

Spider Web table lamp, c. 1899–1918
Tiffany Studios, New York
Leaded Favrile glass

Pomegranate   BOX 6099, ROHNERT PARK, CA 94927

The Charles Hosmer Morse
Museum of American Art

Parrots window, c. 1905
Louis Comfort Tiffany (1848–1933)
Leaded Favrile glass

Pomegranate BOX 6099, ROHNERT PARK, CA 94927

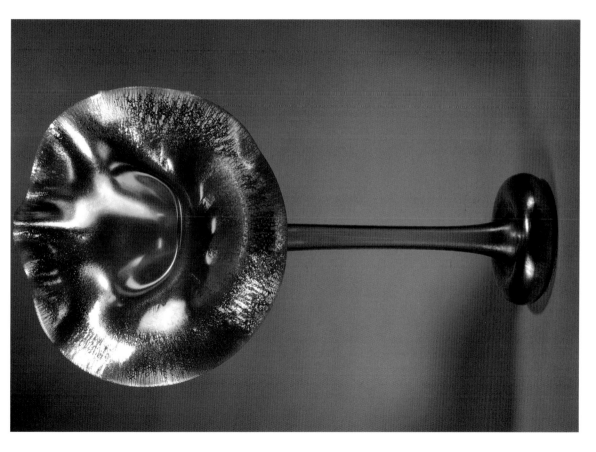

The Charles Hosmer Morse
Museum of American Art

Jack-in-the-Pulpit vase, c. 1901
Louis Comfort Tiffany (1848–1933)
Blown and molded Favrile glass

Pomegranate · BOX 6099, ROHNERT PARK, CA 94927

Tiffany
The Charles Hosmer Morse
Museum of American Art

Picking Gourds window, c. 1897
Designed by Frank Brangwyn (British, 1857–1956) for
Tiffany Glass & Decorating Company, New York
Leaded Favrile glass

Pomegranate BOX 6099, ROHNERT PARK, CA 94927

The Charles Hosmer Morse
Museum of American Art

Autumn, from *Four Seasons* window, c. 1899
Louis Comfort Tiffany (1848–1933)
Leaded Favrile glass

Pomegranate

BOX 6099, ROHNERT PARK, CA 94927

The Charles Hosmer Morse
Museum of American Art

Detail from *Wisteria* window, c. 1910
Designed by Louis Comfort Tiffany (1848–1933)
for Laurelton Hall, his Long Island, New York,
summer home
Leaded Favrile glass

BOX 6099, ROHNERT PARK, CA 94927

Pomegranate

The Charles Hosmer Morse
Museum of American Art

Vase, c. 1900
Louis Comfort Tiffany (1848–1933)
Blown Favrile glass

BOX 6099, ROHNERT PARK, CA 94927

Pomegranate

Tiffany

The Charles Hosmer Morse
Museum of American Art

Aurora window, c. 1894
Louis Comfort Tiffany (1848–1933)
Tiffany Glass & Decorating Co., New York,
after a painting by Will Low (1853–1932)
Leaded Favrile glass

Pomegranate   BOX 6099, ROHNERT PARK, CA 94927

Medallion window, c. 1892
Louis Comfort Tiffany (1848–1933)
Leaded glass

Pomegranate · BOX 6099, ROHNERT PARK, CA 94927

Tiffany

The Charles Hosmer Morse
Museum of American Art

Detail from *Grape Arbor* window, after 1908
Tiffany Studios, New York
Leaded Favrile glass

Tiffany

The Charles Hosmer Morse
Museum of American Art

Dragonfly table lamp, c. 1910
Designed by Clara Driscoll for
Tiffany Studios, New York
Leaded Favrile glass, bronze

Pomegranate   BOX 6099, ROHNERT PARK, CA 94927

Tiffany
The Charles Hosmer Morse
Museum of American Art

Field of Lilies window, c. 1892
Louis Comfort Tiffany (1848–1933)
Leaded Favrile glass

BOX 6099, ROHNERT PARK, CA 94927

Pomegranate

Tiffany
The Charles Hosmer Morse
Museum of American Art

Winter, from *Four Seasons* window, c. 1899
Louis Comfort Tiffany (1848–1933)
Leaded Favrile glass

BOX 6099, ROHNERT PARK, CA 94927

Pomegranate

Tiffany

The Charles Hosmer Morse
Museum of American Art

Aquamarine vase, c. 1910
Louis Comfort Tiffany (1848–1933)
Blown glass

BOX 6099, ROHNERT PARK, CA 94927

Pomegranate

Tiffany

The Charles Hosmer Morse
Museum of American Art

Butterfly window, c. 1885
Louis Comfort Tiffany (1848–1933)
Tiffany Glass Company, New York
Leaded Favrile glass

BOX 6099, ROHNERT PARK, CA 94927

Pomegranate

The Charles Hosmer Morse
Museum of American Art

Cypriot vase, c. 1900
Louis Comfort Tiffany (1848–1933)
Blown Favrile glass

BOX 6099, ROHNERT PARK, CA 94927

Pomegranate

Tiffany

The Charles Hosmer Morse
Museum of American Art

Summer, from *Four Seasons* window, c. 1899
Louis Comfort Tiffany (1848–1933)
Leaded Favrile glass

Pomegranate   BOX 6099, ROHNERT PARK, CA 94927

Tiffany · The Charles Hosmer Morse Museum of American Art

Wisteria lamp, c. 1902
Louis Comfort Tiffany (1848–1933)
Tiffany Studios, New York
Bronze and Favrile glass

Pomegranate · BOX 6099, ROHNERT PARK, CA 94927

Tiffany
The Charles Hosmer Morse Museum of American Art

Peacock necklace, 1906
Designed by Louis Comfort Tiffany
Gold and semiprecious stones

Pomegranate   BOX 6099, ROHNERT PARK, CA 94927

The Charles Hosmer Morse
Museum of American Art

Spring, from *Four Seasons* window, c. 1899
Louis Comfort Tiffany (1848–1933)
Leaded Favrile glass